ROBOT
INNOVATIONS

SPACE
ROBOTS

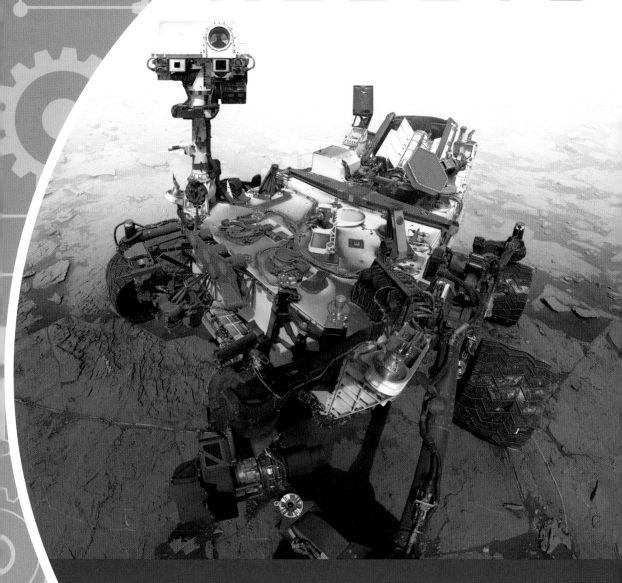

BY ANGIE SMIBERT

CONTENT CONSULTANT
Dr. Joshua Colwell
Professor of Physics
University of Central Florida

Core Library

An Imprint of Abdo Publishing
abdopublishing.com

Cover image: The *Curiosity* rover explores Gale Crater
on Mars.

abdopublishing.com

Published by Abdo Publishing, a division of ABDO, PO Box 398166, Minneapolis, Minnesota 55439. Copyright © 2019 by Abdo Consulting Group, Inc. International copyrights reserved in all countries. No part of this book may be reproduced in any form without written permission from the publisher. Core Library™ is a trademark and logo of Abdo Publishing.

Printed in the United States of America, North Mankato, Minnesota
052018
092018

Cover Photo: JPL-Caltech/MSSS/NASA
Interior Photos: JPL-Caltech/MSSS/NASA, 1, 22, 30 (top), 30 (bottom); NASA, 4–5, 7, 13, 18–19, 24, 32; Sovfoto/Universal Images Group/Getty Images, 10–11; NASA/UPI/Newscom, 14; SVF2/Sovfoto/Universal Images Group/Getty Images, 21; JPL-Caltech/NASA, 28–29, 36–37; JSC/NASA, 34; JPL-Caltech/Arizona State Univ./Space Systems Loral/Peter Rubin/NASA, 40

Editor: Bradley Cole
Imprint Designer: Maggie Villaume
Series Design Direction: Ryan Gale

Library of Congress Control Number: 2017962833

Publisher's Cataloging-in-Publication Data

Names: Smibert, Angie, author.
Title: Space robots / by Angie Smibert.
Description: Minneapolis, Minnesota : Abdo Publishing, 2019. | Series: Robot innovations | Includes online resources and index.
Identifiers: ISBN 9781532114717 (lib.bdg.) | ISBN 9781532154546 (ebook)
Subjects: LCSH: Robots exploring space--Juvenile literature. | Space robotics--Juvenile literature. | Astronautics--Robot applications--Juvenile literature. | Robots--Juvenile literature.
Classification: DDC 629.435--dc23

CONTENTS

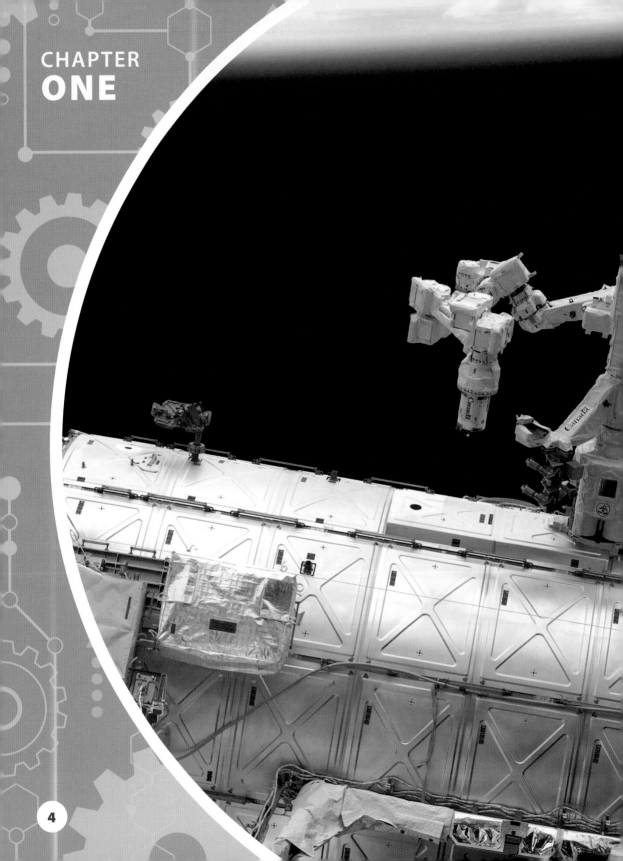

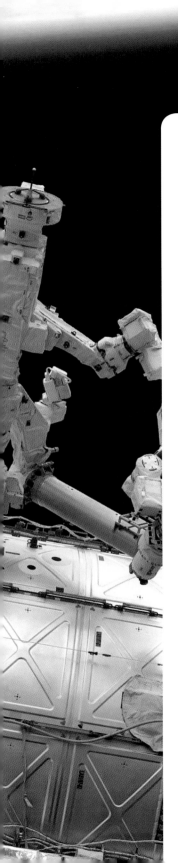

ROBOTS IN SPACE

utside the International Space Station (ISS), a robot named Dextre grabs a battery from a storage area. The two-armed robot spins around through space. He snaps the battery into its slot. The robotic handyman has just changed some of the station's batteries. They power the ISS when its solar panels are not in direct sunlight. Dextre's full name is the Special Purpose Dexterous Manipulator. The robot joined the ISS crew in 2008. Its job is to do repairs outside the station. It also helps unload cargo.

Dextre helps astronauts with jobs outside the space station.

Dextre isn't the only robot in space. Several robots work on the ISS. Humans have been using robots to explore the solar system for decades. Robotic explorers have been to every planet in the solar system. There have been 20 robotic missions to Mars alone.

DESIGNING ROBOTS

DEXTRE

Dextre was designed by the Canadian Space Agency. It is part of the ISS's Mobile Servicing System. This robotic system moves equipment and supplies around the station. Other parts of this system include a large robotic arm, the Canadarm2. Dextre can attach itself to this arm. Its own arms have seven joints that can move in almost any direction. Its hands are grippers with multiple tools. Dextre can use other equipment, such as an external leak detection tool.

WHAT IS A ROBOT?

A robot is a machine that can be programmed to do tasks. Some robots are operated remotely. Others make decisions on their own. They make these choices based on their programming and the world around them. Robots that can make

Robots are important partners for astronauts.

decisions like this have artificial intelligence (AI). Space robots include robotic arms, robotic spacecraft, and even humanoid robots.

WHY USE ROBOTS IN SPACE?

Robots can go where humans can't go. Robotic explorers can spend years flying through space.

ROBOTIC SPACECRAFT

Robotic spacecraft include orbiters, landers, and rovers. Orbiters fly to a planet, then slow down. They enter a planet's orbit. Then they can study it for months or even years. Landers and rovers travel to the surface of a planet or moon. Landers stay in one place. They collect samples and take photos. Rovers can do these things too. But they also can drive from place to place. Scientists can learn more about the planet or moon this way.

They don't need air, food, or water. They can survive extreme heat and cold. Robots can collect and study samples from planets, moons, comets, and asteroids.

Robots can make life easier for people in space. They can unload heavy cargo. Robots can spend days in space making repairs. They also can do boring tasks such as change air filters or move cargo. National Aeronautics and Space Administration (NASA) designers face many challenges. But over the last 50 years, they have learned a lot. The future of space robotics is bright.

STRAIGHT TO THE
SOURCE

Roger Launius works with the National Air and Space Museum. In 2008, he discussed human and robotic space exploration in an interview:

Humans have great capability for problem solving and creativity. And when they're faced with something that's out of the ordinary, that they haven't trained for or plotted out in detail, they can often figure out a way to solve the problem. That's not true with most robots. Yet that may change. . . . But we're not there yet. On the other hand, humans are enormously fragile, and the space environment is instant death to us, while robots are quite hardy and becoming more so all the time.

Source: Tony Reichardt. "Humans vs. Robots." *Air & Space*. Smithsonian, June 26, 2008. Web. Accessed November 21, 2017.

Back It Up

Launius uses examples to make a point about exploration. Write a paragraph describing the point the author is making. Then write down two or three pieces of evidence or examples the author uses to make his point.

EARLY
MISSIONS

Robots have gone where no person has gone before. In fact, most missions to space are done by robots. More than 1,000 robotic spacecraft have been launched in the past 60 years. Those craft have visited every planet in the solar system. Robots have even made it to interstellar space. Some probes and rovers look for life on planets such as Mars.

THE MOON

Some of the earliest robotic missions were to Earth's moon. Starting in the late 1950s, both the United States and the Soviet Union raced

The Soviet Union's *Luna 9* probe sent images from the moon and was a key part of the space race.

to the moon. In 1959, the Soviet *Luna 3* spacecraft took pictures of the dark side of the moon from orbit. The US probe *Ranger 7* transmitted pictures before crashing on the lunar surface in 1964. On February 3, 1966, the Soviet Union landed *Luna 9*. It was the first successful landing of any craft on the moon.

THE INNER PLANETS

Robotic spacecraft also have explored Venus, Mercury, and Mars. In 1962, NASA's *Mariner 2* passed within about 21,000 miles (34,000 km) of Venus. It sent back the first data on Venus's atmosphere. The temperature there is about 900 degrees Fahrenheit (500°C). From 1970 to 1983, the Soviet Union sent the Venera and Vega probes to Venus. On December 15, 1970, *Venera 7* became the first robotic craft to land on another planet. The probe was designed to handle the the hot surface of Venus. It used a parachute to land. It was designed for a hard impact. The shell had no holes or seems keeping heat from getting inside the probe.

Mariner 2 was the second spacecraft of the Mariner program from NASA. It transmitted data about Venus back to Earth.

In the 1960s and 1970s, NASA sent several missions to Mars. *Mariner 9* orbited Mars for a year. It sent back amazing photographs in 1971. The craft mapped about 80 percent of the planet's surface. In 1976, NASA landed *Viking 1* and *Viking 2* on Mars. The landers did experiments and sent data and images to Earth. It was almost 20 years before the next mission to Mars.

In 1996, NASA launched a new program to explore Mars. The *Mars Global Surveyor* is an orbiter that studies Mars's atmosphere from orbit. *Mars Pathfinder* rover landed on July 4, 1997. It explored Mars's terrain.

Voyager 1 launched aboard a Titan IIIE rocket on September 5, 1977.

Spirit and *Opportunity* rovers landed in 2004. They discovered evidence that Mars once had water. The *Curiosity* rover landed in 2012. It was still exploring the Gale Crater in 2018.

THE OUTER PLANETS

In the 1960s, NASA launched several Pioneer missions. *Pioneer 10* was the first spacecraft to pass through the asteroid belt between Mars and Jupiter. The spacecraft took pictures around Jupiter and Saturn. It then headed toward the outer regions of the solar system.

The Voyager mission launched in 1977. *Voyager 1* and *Voyager 2* toured the outer planets. *Voyager 1* and *2* discovered Jupiter's ring system, a moon, and volcanoes on Jupiter's moon Io.

MARTIAN SAND TRAPS

The *Opportunity* rover got stuck in sand in 2005. NASA had hoped to cover a lot of ground. So they put *Opportunity* in a blind drive mode. This means the rover drives forward without looking for obstacles or checking traction. The rover got stuck in a sand dune while in blind-drive mode. It took five weeks to get the rover out of the sand dunes. But the rover got back on track.

Voyager 1 flew by Saturn and explored Saturn's moon, Titan. Then Saturn's gravity flung *Voyager 1* away from the other planets. *Voyager 2* flew by Jupiter, Saturn, Uranus, and Neptune. It took the first close-up photos of these worlds.

DESIGNING ROBOTS

ROBONAUT 2'S CLIMBING LEGS

In 2014, R2 got new legs. They have seven joints. These give the robot more flexibility. Each leg also has an effector on its end. This means R2 can grab onto handholds and other surfaces as it climbs. R2 also can be used with a wheeled base called the Centaur 2. It would make R2 very mobile on a planet or moon's surface.

On August 25, 2012, *Voyager 1* passed through the heliopause. This is the outer boundary around the solar system. *Voyager 1* had entered into interstellar space.

In the 2000s, space agencies began to use humanoid robots in space. Robonaut 2 (R2) joined the crew of the ISS in 2011. R2 is made to work beside people inside or outside the station. The robot has human-like hands. It can use the same tools as astronauts. Its torso can be attached to workbenches. The robot can be controlled remotely or can operate on its own.

STRAIGHT TO THE
SOURCE

Steve Squyres, a scientist in charge of the Mars rover program, talked in an interview about his favorite memory of the *Spirit* rover:

I think my most vivid memories are of the first winter. I never expected Spirit *to survive even one winter on Mars; her landing site was just too far from the equator, and the winters were too harsh. . . .* Spirit *survived that winter by working up the steep north face of Husband Hill, tilting her solar arrays toward the Sun and keeping the power levels up.*

A rover we never expected to survive a Martian winter spent her first winter not just surviving, but doing the first mountaineering on another planet.

Source: Mike Wall. "Remembering Spirit: Q & A With Mars Rover Chief Steve Squyres." *Space.com*. Space.com, May 28, 2011. Web. Accessed February 7, 2018.

Consider Your Audience

Adapt this passage for a different audience, such as your friends. Write a blog post conveying the same information for the new audience. How does your post differ from the original text and why?

CHALLENGES OF SPACE

Space travel is challenging. Temperatures range from blazing hot to freezing cold. Some planets have high pressures and toxic gases. Others have thin atmospheres and are hit by the Sun's rays. All these conditions create unique problems. Engineers must find solutions. Fixing a distant spacecraft is impossible, so these robots must be built to last.

GRAVITY

Spacecraft in orbit are affected by gravity. They are falling toward Earth, but they fall so quickly

Spacecraft are covered in reflective blankets to both hold heat in and reflect solar radiation.

that they match the curve of the earth. Robots on the ISS are falling at the same speed as the station, so they appear to float. A robot such as Robonaut 2 needs a way to move itself along. It also needs a way to anchor itself to do work.

The strength of gravity on a planet or moon depends on its mass. But the moon and Mars are much smaller than Earth. They have weaker gravity. An object on the moon weighs about one-sixth what it would on Earth. On Mars, an object weighs about one-third of its

DESIGNING ROBOTS

HEDGEHOG ROBOTS

NASA's Jet Propulsion Laboratory designed the Hedgehog robot. It may one day tumble its way across a low-gravity asteroid. The robot is basically a cube with spikes. Inside the cube, a flywheel spins and brakes to make the robot hop. It can move no matter which side of the cube is up. The spikes act as feet. Spikes keep the robot from floating off and protect the cube from the terrain. The spikes could also house instruments, such as thermal probes.

Venera 7 was exposed to the extreme heat of the Venus atmosphere and malfunctioned.

Earth weight. This can be a good thing. A rover on Mars does not need to be strong. The planet's gentler gravity means the rover can be lightweight.

Asteroids and comets are much smaller than planets. They have extremely weak gravity. The *Philae* lander touched down on comet 67P in 2014. The comet's gravity is 10,000 times weaker than Earth's gravity. Objects can float away into space. *Philae* tried to hook itself to the comet. But this system failed. The lander bounced twice before stopping. These bounces took more than two hours.

TEMPERATURE

Robotic spacecraft face extreme temperatures. On the moon, there is no atmosphere to keep the temperature steady. It can reach about 250 degrees Fahrenheit (120°C) in sunlight. It can drop to about -270 degrees Fahrenheit (-170°C) in the shade. Venus has a thick atmosphere. It traps heat and warms up the planet. The temperature has measured as hot as 864 degrees Fahrenheit (462°C). Extreme cold can be hard on gears and metal parts. It can freeze

Curiosity drilled samples at the Mojave site on Mars while under remote control from Earth.

VOYAGER 2

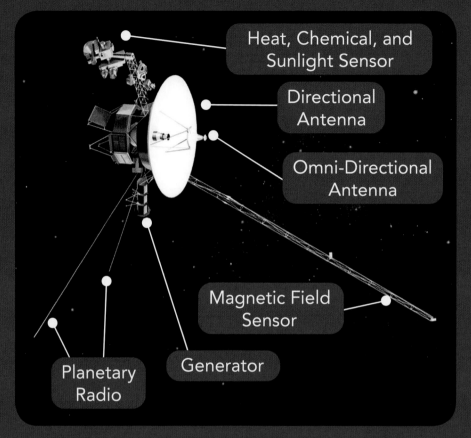

Heat, Chemical, and Sunlight Sensor

Directional Antenna

Omni-Directional Antenna

Magnetic Field Sensor

Generator

Planetary Radio

Robotic spacecraft such as *Voyager 2* need lots of parts and sensors to be able to complete their missions. What are some key parts of this probe that help overcome obstacles in space?

fluids and gases. Thermal blankets guard against the cold of space. They are often applied over the craft. To guard against temperature changes, these blankets are reflective. They reflect the heat from the Sun or atmosphere of a planet. This keeps the temperature inside the craft steady. Extreme heat can melt everything. *Venera 7* crash landed on Venus after the extreme heat caused its parachute to fail. It still managed to transmit for 23 minutes from the planet's surface before going silent.

DISTANCE

Most robotic spacecraft orbit Earth. But some spacecraft travel millions of miles from Earth. The radio signals sent to and from spacecraft travel at the speed of light. On Earth, this seems instant, but for longer distances, this creates lag

NASA'S DEEP SPACE NETWORK

The Deep Space Network (DSN) tracks missions and communicates with spacecraft. The DSN is made up of three giant radio antenna arrays. They are located in California, Spain, and Australia. Each site has multiple antennae with sensitive receivers. They can pick up weak signals from distant craft, including the *Voyagers*. These three facilities are located approximately 120 degrees apart on Earth. This enables one facility to be in contact with a spacecraft at all times. This network allows NASA to monitor missions, receive information from probe sensors, and even send commands to crafts.

when communicating with the spacecraft. The lag grows as a robot gets farther from Earth. Signals take about a second and a half to get to the moon. Depending on how far Earth and Mars are from each other the lag can be much worse. From Earth to Mars, the lag can be 13 minutes. And signals have to travel back to Earth. This means the *Curiosity* rover sometimes has 26 minutes of lag. This lag can cause problems.

POWER

Robots need power. Missions end when a spacecraft can no longer run its instruments or call home. Most probes, landers, and rovers use solar panels. These devices turn sunlight into electricity. These devices work well in the inner solar system. The Sun's rays are strong enough to provide plenty of power.

Long-range craft need another option. They use an electric generator powered by materials such as plutonium. The plutonium naturally produces heat. That heat is converted to electricity to power the craft.

HUMANS

A new challenge for space robots is working with humans. Today, they work together on the ISS. In the future, they may team up on a planet or moon. Robots still will do the more dangerous tasks. They may help build structures. They can fix equipment in space. The robot might need to be able to use the same tools that a human does. This is why NASA is developing humanoid robots, such as Robonaut 2 and Valkyrie.

FURTHER EVIDENCE

Chapter Three included information about some of the challenges space robots face. Review the chapter to find evidence for one of those challenges, such as gravity or temperatures. Then explore the Robonaut 2 page and find a passage that discusses one of those challenges and how the designers tackled it.

abdocorelibrary.com/space-robots

SPACE ROBOTS IN ACTION

The *Curiosity* rover landed on Mars on August 5, 2012. Its mission is to look for evidence that Mars could have once had life. *Curiosity* is the size of a small SUV. It is a moving laboratory. *Curiosity* has 17 cameras and a robotic arm. The rover has 10 scientific instruments. *Curiosity* captures images, tests samples, and relays data as it explores the Gale Crater. It can use a laser to vaporize rocks up to 23 feet (7 m) away. Then a special camera analyzes the vapor. It looks for elements that are critical to life.

Curiosity used a new landing method to safely descend to the Martian surface.

CURIOSITY ROVER

Curiosity is a rover designed to explore Gale Crater on Mars. It has six wheels. The rover's head and mast carry seven cameras. At the end of its arm, *Curiosity* has a turret (or "hand"). The turret carries a drill, dust brush, soil scoop, close-up camera, and two other scientific instruments. How might these tools help it explore Mars' environment?

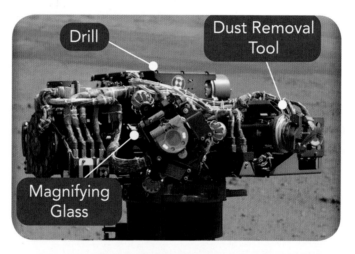

Drill

Dust Removal Tool

Magnifying Glass

Collection and Handling for Interior Martian Rock Analysis

Alpha Particle X-Ray Spectrometer

Curiosity used its chemical camera to test these vapors. It found evidence that Mars could have once been suited for life. *Curiosity* continues to look for life. The rover found carbon in rocks. Carbon makes up organic matter, such as plants. The robot found signs of an ancient streambed and liquid salt water underneath the surface. Liquid water is essential for life.

CASSINI

The *Cassini-Huygens* spacecraft was launched on October 15, 1997. It had two parts. *Cassini* was a NASA orbiter. It would

DESIGNING ROBOTS

CURIOSITY'S SKY CRANE

Landing an SUV-sized rover softly on Mars was a huge challenge. NASA engineers designed a system they called the Sky Crane to gently lower the rover to the surface. The Sky Crane is a hovering platform with rocket engines at each corner. *Curiosity* was attached underneath. Once both entered the atmosphere, a parachute slowed them down. Then the Sky Crane's engines fired, slowing it down to a hover. It lowered *Curiosity* on a cable. Once on the ground, *Curiosity* cut the cable.

Cassini was designed to explore Saturn and carry the *Huygens* probe to Titan.

study Saturn and its moons. *Huygens* was a lander

created by the European Space Agency (ESA). It would

land on one of Saturn's moons, Titan.

On July 1, 2004, *Cassini* arrived at Saturn. The robotic craft observed the planet until 2017. During its long life, *Cassini* made amazing discoveries. In 2005, *Cassini* spotted fractures in the icy crust of Enceladus, Saturn's sixth largest moon. Later flybys revealed a water vapor cloud over the moon. This means Enceladus has cryovolcanoes under its crust. Cryovolcanoes spew jets of water and ice instead of lava. On Enceladus, they shoot water and ice into space. *Cassini* sampled this material. The sample led researchers to believe that Enceladus has an ocean under its icy crust.

HUYGENS

On January 14, 2005, the *Huygens* probe made history's most distant landing on a solid surface. *Cassini* released *Huygens* near Titan. The probe coasted toward the moon for 21 days. A hard shell protected *Huygens* as it fell into Titan's atmosphere. A parachute slowed its landing. The lander included six scientific instruments. It took photos and sent back data for two hours before its batteries ran out.

SPHERES perform experiments aboard the ISS that are submitted by middle school students.

SPHERES AND ASTROBEE

Three volleyball-sized robots float on the ISS. The Synchronized Position Hold Engage and Reorient Experimental Satellite (SPHERES) systems arrived at the ISS in 2006. These robots use tiny blasts of carbon dioxide to move around in zero gravity. Sensors help them navigate through the station. Astronauts use the floating robots to conduct experiments. They are designed to test programs for spacecraft, orbiting telescopes, and satellites. Students can write and test instructions for the robots in computer code.

Astrobee is the newest generation of flying robot used on the ISS. The Astrobee is a one-foot (30.5-cm) cube with a camera. It was designed to help test technologies in zero gravity. The Astrobee helps astronauts with their chores. It also provides mission controllers with eyes and ears on the ISS.

EXPLORE ONLINE

Chapter Four discusses several robots that are or were used to explore the solar system, including the *Curiosity* rover. Examine NASA's Mars Exploration Program site. Compare and contrast the information found on *Curiosity* with information found in this book.

MARS EXPLORATION PROGRAM
abdocorelibrary.com/space-robots

THE FUTURE: MARS AND BEYOND

NASA plans to return to Mars in 2020. It will send a new robotic rover. The mission will be to find a place for astronauts to live. *Mars 2020* will carry on that quest to different parts of Mars. The site for *Mars 2020* has yet to be chosen.

The new rover will be based on *Curiosity*. But it will have new and improved equipment. *Mars 2020* will drill into Mars for samples that will be returned to Earth. Other changes include more durable wheels and microphones for listening to the landing. The Sky Crane will

Mars 2020 is planned to take off during the summer of 2020.

be used for landing. It hovers using rocket engines and will lower the rover with a tether. The rover also will test a system for making oxygen out of the carbon dioxide found on Mars. This is a key step in helping human explorers use the planet's resources to survive.

HUMANOID ROBOTS

NASA is also developing a new robot for Mars. Valkyrie is a six-foot, two-inch (1.8 m) humanoid robot. It's covered in an armor-like material. It was originally designed for a search-and-rescue contest. NASA lent two Valkyries to universities. They are working to get it ready for Mars.

Engineers hope the robot will help humans explore Mars.

VALKYRIE

NASA's Valkyrie R5 robot was originally designed for the Defense Advanced Research Projects Agency (DARPA) contest in 2013 and was built in just 15 months. After the contest, NASA sent a Valkyrie to Northeastern University in Boston and another Valkyrie to Massachusetts Institute of Technology (MIT) for testing. It has been designed to work with humans and by itself.

Valkyrie would arrive on Mars before humans. The robot would then build living and work spaces. Once humans arrive, it would help maintain the habitat and explore the surface.

EXPLORING ASTEROIDS

In the near future, several space agencies and companies plan to send robotic spacecraft to asteroids. Some missions are just for research. NASA's OSIRIS-REx launched in September 2016.

DESIGNING ROBOTS

ORIGAMI ROBOTS

Origami is the Japanese art of folding paper into special shapes. Some new robots have been inspired by this. They can fold themselves into various shapes. Their new shape helps them complete their missions. NASA's wheeled scout robot is called PUFFER. It is designed to get into and out of tight spaces. PUFFER, which stands for Pop-Up Flat Folding Explorer Robot, has two rugged wheels that can move over rough terrain. The robot can also flatten itself. While flattened it can crawl under or through obstacles. Several robots can also be flattened and stacked. This makes them easier to store. A rover might have a pack of PUFFERs on board.

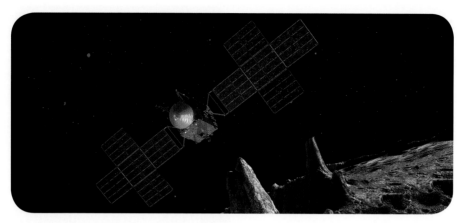

Psyche, launching in 2022, will be exploring a metal asteroid.

Its mission is to collect debris from Bennu, a near-Earth asteroid. A sampler will capture debris blown off the surface. The sampler will approach Bennu in July 2020. The robotic craft will bring back what it has collected for study in 2023.

NASA also plans to explore asteroids that are farther away. In 2025, *Lucy* will visit the main asteroid belt and several Trojan asteroids. These asteroids share Jupiter's orbit with the Sun. Another robotic craft, *Psyche*, will orbit 16 Psyche, one of the largest asteroids in the main asteroid belt. This asteroid appears to once have been the metal core of a planet. Scientist hope to learn about the cores of planets by studying it.

ASTEROID MINING

Several companies have plans to mine asteroids in the near future. Robotic craft could extract water as well as precious metals from asteroids. Those metals could range from iron and nickel to rarer metals, such as platinum and palladium.

A robot might drill out these resources and send them back to Earth. Or the robot could send the ore or water to a space station or even Mars. For a colony on Mars, getting materials from asteroids could be cheaper than having them sent from Earth. In the long run, asteroid mining could help open space exploration.

Robots have been a key part of space exploration. With new rovers, probes, and folding robots, robots will continue to explore planets and even interstellar space. With information gathered by previous robots, engineers can build more capable robots to do even more new tasks and hold key roles in future missions.

FAST FACTS

- Robots are machines that can be programmed to do tasks.

- Space robots include robotic spacecraft as well as humanoid robots that work alongside people.

- Experts have debated whether space exploration should be carried out by robots, humans, or both.

- Several robots are at work on the International Space Station, including Robonaut 2, SPHERES, and Dextre.

- *Cassini* discovered many amazing things about Saturn and its moons. Enceladus, for instance, has an ocean underneath its icy crust.

- *Curiosity* has discovered water and evidence that ancient Mars could have supported life. The rover is still making discoveries on Mars.

- Space robots face many challenges in space, including low gravity, rough terrain, extreme temperatures, and power.

- Most robotic spacecraft use either solar panels or a nuclear generator for power.

- NASA's Deep Space Network tracks and communicates with interplanetary spacecraft.

- NASA is developing a humanoid robot to work on Mars alongside humans.

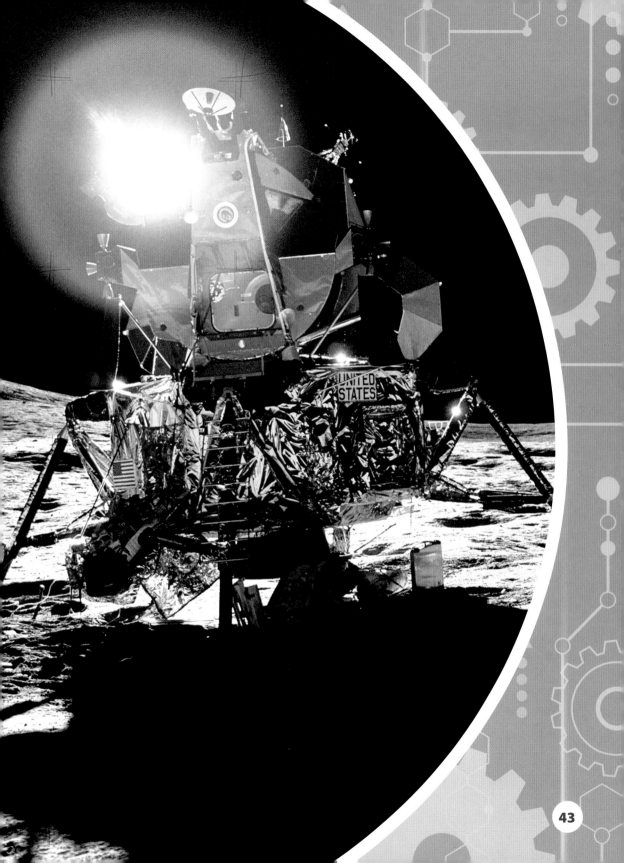

STOP AND
THINK

Tell the Tale

Chapter Five of this book discusses a humanoid robot designed to one day prepare Mars for human colonists. Imagine you are one of these colonists. Write 200 words about what you have to do to once you arrive on Mars. How does the robot help you? How do you feel about working alongside it?

Dig Deeper

After reading this book, what questions do you still have about using humanoid robots in space? Find a few reliable sources to help you answer your questions.

Why Do I Care?

Perhaps you're not interested in space exploration. But that doesn't mean you can't imagine how robots in space may affect life on Earth. How might the challenges faced by space robot engineers apply to robots used on Earth?

Another View

This book talks about the history of robotic exploration of planets such as Mars. As you know, every source is different. Ask a librarian to help you find another source about the history of robotic space exploration. Write a short essay comparing and contrasting the new source's point of view with that of this book's author. What is the point of view of each author? How are they similar? How are they different and why?

GLOSSARY

asteroid
a small, rocky body that orbits around the Sun

atmosphere
the layer of gases surrounding a planet or moon

effector
a device at the end of a robotic arm

flywheel
a heavy revolving wheel in a machine

heliopause
the boundary between the solar system and interstellar space

interstellar
between stars

orbit
a path that an object such as a planet or satellite takes around another object

satellite
an artificial body orbiting a planet or moon

sensor
a device that detects or measures a physical property, such as temperature

ONLINE RESOURCES

To learn more about space robots, visit our free resource websites below.

Core Library
CONNECTION
FREE! COMMON CORE MULTIMEDIA RESOURCES

Visit **abdocorelibrary.com** for free Common Core resources for teachers and students, including vetted activities, multimedia, and booklinks, for deeper subject comprehension.

Booklinks
NONFICTION NETWORK
FREE! ONLINE NONFICTION RESOURCES

Visit **abdobooklinks.com** for free additional online weblinks for further learning. These links are routinely monitored and updated to provide the most current information available.

LEARN MORE

Hamilton, S. L. *Robots & Rovers*. Minneapolis, MN: Abdo Publishing, 2011.

Koontz, Robin. *Robotics in the Real World*. Minneapolis, MN: Abdo Publishing, 2015.

INDEX

About the Author

Angie Smibert is the author of several young adult and middle grade science fiction and fantasy novels. She has also written numerous educational titles. She was also a writer and online training developer at NASA's Kennedy Space Center for many, many years. She received NASA's prestigious Silver Snoopy as well as several other awards for her work.